Abraham Messler

Sermons and Tributes of Respect on the Occasion of the

Death of Hon. Peter D. Vroom

Abraham Messler

Sermons and Tributes of Respect on the Occasion of the Death of Hon. Peter D. Vroom

ISBN/EAN: 9783337098414

Printed in Europe, USA, Canada, Australia, Japan

Cover: Foto ©Lupo / pixelio.de

More available books at **www.hansebooks.com**

SERMONS

AND

TRIBUTES OF RESPECT

ON THE OCCASION OF THE DEATH OF THE

HON. PETER D. VROOM,

EX-GOVERNOR OF THE STATE OF NEW JERSEY.

BY

REV. ABRAHAM MESSLER, D. D.,

SOMERVILLE, N. J., 1874.

———— ◆ ————

SOMERVILLE, N. J.
J. R. SCHENK—MESSENGER—PRINTER.
1874.

FUNERAL SERMON.

"Knowing in ourselves that ye have in Heaven, a better and more en-during substance."—Heb. x. 34.

The persons referred to were sufferers, and took joyfully the "spoiling of their goods," because they *knew* that in a better world they had a better and more enduring substance; *i. e.*, their assurance of a blessed life in the future, enabled them to endure patiently—even joyfully, the worst evils of the present, in order to attain it. So it is always. The hope of immortal blessedness throws its radiance back upon the darkest hours of human life, and makes their sorrows less. We can part with all things cheerfully—even with life itself—when we know that we have a glori-ous life assured to us in Heaven, waiting our coming, and possession. We remark therefore—

I. There is a state of future blessedness prepared for Christians in Heaven. This is taken for granted in the words of our text, rather than directly affirmed ; and it is a fact that all men, in some way, entertain this belief. It has been shaddowed forth in every religious creed, in more or less clearness, in all time. It seems indeed, to be, in some sense, a human instinct. It roots itself in a Christian's consciousness, as one of his clearest, strongest and most abiding convictions. He regards the provision of it as being one of the grandest results of Christ's work in dying for men, and he believes in his own future enjoyment of it, as one of the greatest blessings which Christ promises to those who receive him and believe in his name. His faith in Christ enables him to "read his title clear, to mansions in the skies," and to feel that those mansions are to be his home.

II. The enjoyments of this state of immortal blessedness are "*real*, being a better and more enduring substance." Not material indeed, but still, just as real as if actually formed out of material things. Spiritual being is as *real* as being, as mortal being is, or can possibly be ! God is a spirit, angels are spirits, the human soul is a spirit and each one of these has an existence as true and as real, as any material organization or creation can have.

This *substantive reality* is put here, in opposition to visions, imaginations, surmisings, or expectations. The fact is, Heaven, as a state and a life, is just as real as the earth, and our life here is. Our not *seeing* it, and its being reserved as a manifestation of the future, is no reason why we should doubt it : for in truth, and in fact, the glory of it lies all around us in a thousand beautiful forms, and the human soul, just when bursting away from its earthly fetters, often has a vision of it : which in brightness is like rapture—a foretaste and an antepast, given in assurance and of what is waiting and will be enjoyed in perfect fulness when we have come to the heavenly state.

III Heaven is a *better* substance. There are many good things kindly given us in our earthly life. Oh how many there are ! and how gracious God is in giving them in such profusion ; but they are not Heaven—not in any form like Heaven ! Heaven is more, is higher, is purer, is more complete. There is no sin, no suffering, no death in Heaven. The soul is not fettered there, as it always is here ; but free to rise up in grateful adoration and praise, even to the very highest note. It is near God ; it sees God, and it experiences and knows the full glory of that high estate. There are no weaknesses, interruptions, distractions or preventions to mar its perfect joy. It has attained ; it is at home and at rest ! In every way—in all senses, Heaven, as a state of enjoyment and a condition of life, is *infinitely better* than the world can ever be ; and this is not disparaging what we possess now : it is only properly exalting what is to come, and what we shall realize when we are at home with the saints in Heaven.

IV. Heaven is a more *enduring* substance. The eternal years of God belong to, and are absorbed in the Heavenly life ; and it goes on rising up from one degree to another, until the fulness of absolute perfection is attained, which is described as "a fashioning into the divine image," and a passing on from "glory to glory." What such words import, waits the future revelations of the Heavenly state to interpret and make manifest to us fully. We may therefore cheer our desponding hours here, by singing :

Rejoice, Oh grieving heart,
    The hours fly fast ;
With each some sorrow dies,
With each some shadow flies,
    Until at last
The dawning in the East
Bids weary night depart,
    And pain is ever past!

V. We can *know in ourselves* that we have in
Heaven a better and more enduring substance ! This sup-
poses that religious sentiment and consciousness is real not
only, but that it is the best and highest evidence of the
certainty of our future hopes ; and is it not so ? If we
are conscious and know in ourselves anything pertaining to
sentiment, enjoyment, and experience, can we have any
better evidence of its reality ? Religion is a sentiment :
and in its practical form and power, it is more a sentiment
than it is anything else ! our experience of its influence is
a reality. We *know in ourselves* that we have had such
an experience and felt such a power. Now, in Scripture,
this is represented as a "regeneration unto life"—as a
"passing from death to life"—as a "new creature"—as
"Christ formed within us the hope of glory !" In its out-
ward manifestations it exhibits itself in a *life*—an all-con-
trolling power, which makes us what we were not, and enables us to live as we would not have lived, but for what has
been effected in us; and this efficient power is not human,
but a manifestation of the gracious influence of the Holy
Spirit.

Now the *life* of religion, and eternal *life* in Heaven, are
only different conditions of the same power, in different

states of being. To have the sentiment of religion deeply impressed upon us—to have a consciousness of it, is therefore to have an earnest and a beginning of Heaven. In other words, we know then *in ourselves* that there is a Heaven, and that in the Heavenly state we shall have a "better and more enduring substance." It is eternal life in its first state and embodies all its future realizations.

I am persuaded that the strength of hope and the triumphant confidence of true piety, is the result chiefly of this inward knowledge ; in other words, belongs to an experience of the reality and the power of the sentiment of religion in the heart ! The martyrs faith and steadfast endurance of every torment, even of death itself, was evidently something more than mere belief in doctrines or an attachment to principles, however important they might be, or be felt to be ! They knew in themselves that they had in Heaven a better and more enduring substance : and hence, neither the spoiling of their goods, nor the presence of a painful death could move them from the sure steadfastness of their confidence. When the choice was, to suffer now or to loose the coming glory, they could not, and did not hesitate for a moment ! The *better* and the *higher* had to be secured at all events: and their deep conviction of its importance and its glory, left them nothing else to do.

Now our departed friend, Peter D. Vroom, had this consciousness. His whole life was a manifestation of the power, the permanency and the pervading influence of religious sentiment. He made a profession of this and united with our Church, on a confession of his faith, 51 years ago

last May, during what we designate as the "Great Revival!"
I found him here, sitting as an elder, when I came to occu-
py the office of pastor, 41 years since. Our confidential intercourse and friendship commenced then, and, has never
been intermitted. He has lived away from us for some of
the last years, but he has ever continued with us in spirit,
and claimed this Church as his religious home! It was
his father's Church. He grew up in it, was early instruct-
ed in its doctrines, and loved it dearly. He first experienced the power of Christian sentiment here ; and the last
words he spake to me were to this effect : "I have been
with you, and am one of you, and I shall be with you," and
then his emotions choked his words, but he meant to say—
"I shall be with you when I am no more." It is right
that he should be brought here, and these last words
spoken of him here, among those who are left of the generation who loved him as a Christian brother, honored him as
a Christian man, and reverenced him, when he sat here an
Elder in the church of God.

Governor Vroom's religious sentiment was far above the
ordinary type. It manifested a decided power and activity.
It pervaded his whole conduct, and became the controlling
element in his daily life ! It produced a conscientious integrity and purity which manifested itself in everything he
said and did, at the bar, in his official capacity as the chief
Executive officer of the State, in his decisions as Chancellor, in Congress, when representing the United
States at the Court in Berlin, and as a Trustee of the
"Sinking Fund." Those who had occasion to transact busi-

ness with him in any and all of these official relations, have ever given but one account of what he was, and what he did. There was even a delicacy in his conscientiousness, and an accuracy in his integrity, which impressed the observant and excited often their surprise and admiration. He would have nothing but what was just, and right, and true, and nothing could entice or swerve him from it.

He was a devotional man ; and manifested its influence, not only on Sabbath during public worship, but in his household, and in his most private hours. I have travelled with him, roomed with him at places of public resort, staid with him in his private family, here and in other lands, and seen ample evidence of this beautiful spirit in every one of these situations. From the time that he made a public profession of the Christian religion, he set up an altar in his house and offered on it daily a sacrifice of prayer and praise. It was with him, something more always, than a mere form. He felt it to be an important duty which he owed to himself and to his household ; while at the same time he enjoyed it as a religious service in which he found uniformly, delight, comfort and strength ; and he was steadfast in this practice to the end of life, as I am sure, from a personal knowledge of the man and a long acquaintance with his sentiments and feelings. His prayers often impressed me as beautiful models of fervent piety and humble childlike faith. They were penitent from a sense of sin, grateful in recognizing the redemption of Christ, and trustful of the promised mercies of a superintending providence, mingled always with earnest supplications for grace, strength, comfort and peace, in all the various trials and temptations of a sinful world ! He seemed to me often when praying, to be the humblest, sincerest, and the most trusting Christian I have ever known.

But with all this childlike *simplicity of character*, he was a strong, and a decided man—very strong in his sense of right, and his resolution to have the right done, and to contend for it unto the very last ; and any man who went about to resist him, needed to be well armed indeed. He prevented in his official and professional life, a vast amount of wrong from being done ; and his memory will be cherished long among all the noble and the good, who had occasion to ask his personal aid in their various difficulties !

He was a grave man, constitutionally inclined to nervous depression ! He suffered from it often acutely. In his last sickness, he was at first peculiarly depressed ! The fear of death was strong upon him, and his mind almost in total darkness. I reasoned with him, apparently with some success. When I left him, he at least seemed to be more composed and trustful. I reminded him that dying grace was not necessary before dying, and expressed a firm belief that it would be given him when needed; and it was ! The gloom passed completely away from his mind, and his hope of Heavenly joy became assured. Every fear and doubt vanished or was removed, and he seemed to those who watched by him, to be perfectly composed and happy. His face, for several days, wore the most radiant expression, and he said : "he wished every one to know how precious Jesus had been to him." This continued as long as the control of his faculties remained unimpaired. Even when from weakness and exhaustion, his memory and reasoning powers were nearly lost to him, he yet constantly appeared, as if he was dwelling upon heavenly things, or was already realizing the joys of the heavenly state. His frequent expression was "Come blessed Jesus," or else, "I want to go home." It was almost a perfect revelation of what has been so graphically sketched by a poet :

> Have we not caught that smiling,
> On some beloved face,
> As if a Heavenly sound were wiling
> The soul from its earthly place?
> The distant sound and sweet,
> Of the Master's coming feet!
> We may clasp the loved one faster,
> And plead for a little while,
> But who can resist the Master?
> And we read by that brightening smile.
> That the tread we may not hear,
> Is drawing surely near—"

It was unquestionably, an expression of the joy within his soul, and the rapture he experienced in communing with Heaven.

The last day or two he seemed to be constantly looking for some one to come and take him away. His recitation of Hymns and Scripture, was wonderful. His whole soul evidently was full of truth ; beautiful truth, and he joyed in it ! The last connected words which could be understood were : "I am going home this morning," and he did go ! Yes, home to the glorious mansions, which our Saviour has assured us, are prepared for *his own* in our Heavenly Father's house.

> Home and at rest
> Like closing flowers at night,
> 'Till Heaven the morn shall bless,
> And bring a brighter light.

Thus dying grace came in rich abundance in dying moments, and he waited only to be called upward.

We have been constrained to dwell to this extent, upon the Christian character of our departed friend. The effect of his noble life must not be lost ; and the finishing touch which his dying hours gave to the piety which he professed and uniformly manifested, was too sweet and precious to be omitted. Our only regret is, that circumstances constrain to such brevity and prevent a full and proper record. The generation of noble, godly statesmen, to which he belonged, is rapidly passing away—too rapidly for the public good, and for the safety of all our important interests He will be remembered as one of our greatest, purest, and noblest men : and New Jersey has a just pride in having given her full quota of such, to public life.

We will carry his remains in a few moments, and deposit them amid kindred dust.

> "Such graves as his, are pilgrim shrines,
> Shrines to no creed or code confined ;
> The Delphian vales, the Palestines,
> The Meccas of the mind."

It is a beautiful spot ; he marked the place himself where he desired to rest. It is near the banks of our smooth flowing river, and not far from the old homestead, where he first breathed the breath of life. He always loved this beautiful river and the valley through which it flows, with a kind of childlike affection. It seemed to be his beau-ideal of rural beauty, and social and moral excellency. Its memories were garnered among his treasured stores. I often thought he must have spent a very happy youth. He seemed to dwell so lovingly upon its scenes. His early associates, the men of the past, his youthful aspirations, and the beginnings of his public life, were constantly reverted to, with a fondness that was never weary of repetition and never seemed to be exhausted. He appeared often to be saying to himself as he thought of it :

On thy calm joys, with what delight I dream,
Thou dear green valley, of my native stream :
Fancy still waves o'er thee, the enchanting wand,
And every nook of thine is fairy land.

When he returned from Berlin, it was his intention to purchase his paternal homestead, on the banks of the Raritan River, fit it up and make it his residence, for at least a part of the year. *There* he would be once more in the very midst of the scenes of his early life. Then he should be able to worship again in this old church, which he loved so much. When he spoke of it, he seemed to feel that when realized, he would be almost young again. But when he came to look at the old homestead, it was so changed ! The fruit trees which he remembered were gone : a grove of tall woodland across the river, which protected it from the cold north winds, had been sacrificed; and what seemed to him almost to be profane hands, had changed the form of the old mansion itself. He turned away and came back saddened and disappointed. It was not the home that he remembered and loved. I think he was very sad, for he never spake of it again.

I have uttered these words concerning our friend, because I felt that I must do it. Even the reserved delicacy of the tenderest hearts which have been listening to me, will justify it. I have dwelt almost exclusively upon his Christian character. This belonged to me as his Pastor and friend. Others can—as they will—speak of his secular and official life. They are only a few words that have been spoken: on a future occasion I intend to speak more fully for the gratification of his friends in this Church, and this community. To me it is one of the saddest bereavements of my whole life. He was for so many years my truest and best friend, and I owe him so much. But he has found rest, and I hope to join him soon.

This is my comfort, and the same comfort remains for his beloved wife and children. There is not one reason why any one of them should mourn, except that he is no more. He lived well, lived long, and attained the noblest end of living. He died in a good old age, full of days, and full of honors, and he rests in God! Oh that we might live so well, and rest so sweetly! It has been truly and beautifully said that "Death is the justification of all the ways of the Christian, the last end of all his sacrifices, that touch of the great master which completes the picture, harmonizing every shade, and giving its true effect to every line and tint "

> We know for us a rest remains,
> When God will give us sweet release
> From earth, and all our mortal chains,
> And turn our sufferings into peace.
> What we have won with pain, we hold more fast,
> What tarrieth long, is sweeter at the last,
>   Be thou content.

MEMORIAL SERMON.

Judges viii 32 : And Gideon, the son of Joash, died in a good old age, and was buried in the Sepulchre of Joash his father.

1st. Chron. 29, 28 : And he—David—died in a good old age, full of days, wishes, and honor.

We have quoted these texts, as examples of good men in official life, who came to old age and honor on account of their integrity, purity and faithfulness. They cover all the ground which we expect to embrace in the present discourse, which is to be occupied with the *life*, the *character*, and the *public services* of one of the oldest and most honored members of this church, recently deceased. He was known and loved by many of a former generation, and ought to be distinguished in this special way by us, because of the many excellencies of his character and his eminence in public life.

Peter D. Vroom was born on the 12th day of December 1791, on the south banks of the Raritan River, near the junction of its two main branches. The old mansion, made by him an historical house, is still standing, almost in the same condition in which it was when he came into life, under its protective roof. His father, Col. Peter D. Vroom, was a man well known and very highly respected in his day ; a Christian man of more than ordinary intelligence and reading : a man who filled several offices of honor and trust in the County and in the State. He assisted in raising the first company of Militia in Hillsborough Township, at the opening of the Revolution, and was in the Battle of Brandywine, commanding it as Lieutenant, after the Captain, Isaac Brokaw, had been slain. He served the County as High Sheriff, and occupied a seat both in the Council and Legislative Assembly for several successive years.

By his mother, Elsie Bogert, Gov. Vroom was lineally descended from Sarah Rapelye, the first white child born on Long Island, and so inherited some of the noble Huguenot blood.

His early life was spent in the old homestead. He was brought up strictly, and early taught the Catechism of our Reformed Dutch Church. He attended school at first in the "Old Red School House," on the river banks, below the crossing at Beekman's Lane ; but in 1806, at 12 years of age, he commenced the study of the Latin and Greek languages, preparatory to a collegiate course, under Jacob Kirkpatrick, in the Somerville Academy; walking daily, and returning the whole distance from his father's house to Somerville. He entered Columbia College as a junior in 1806 and graduated in 1808 with honor, at the early age of seventeen years Almost immediately, he entered the office of George McDonald in Somerville, as a student at law and came to the bar in 1813 after the usual term of study : becoming a Counsellor in 1816, and a Sergeant-at-law in 1828 in due course. He found there, Stockton, Johnson.

Scott, Williamson, the two Frelinghuysens, Frederick and Theodore, as competitors. Young as he was, he took his place among these eminent men, not as an inferior, but as a younger member of an honorable profession, who expected to be their equal in due time.

He commenced the practice of his profession, by opening an office at Schooley's Mountain Springs. A year and a half subsequently, he removed to Hackettstown, in Sussex County, and two years afterwards, to Flemington, in Hunterdon County. He made friends, and gained clients in both these places, who adhered to him as long as they lived. In 1819 he returned to Somerville, and occupied the residence and office of his preceptor, George McDonald, having married on the 21st of May, 1817, Anna Dumont. He had already in these early years, made for himself a reputation for integrity and ability which promised largely, and he soon came to be esteemed one of the most prominent young Barristers in the State. In a short time his eminence was universally acknowledged. Chief Justice Kirkpatrick spoke of him on one occasion, in delivering an opinion from the Bench, as "a Counsellor whose acuteness and accuracy is inferior to none of his standing, at the Bar." He was soon known, not only as an able, but an honest and honorable lawyer. A writer refering to his attainments in mature life, says: "it may safely be said of him, that, occupying as he did, a first position at the bar, there was no practitioner who commanded, by his ability, his sound judgment, and his vast experience, more unlimited confidence and respect:" of no one could it more properly be said, he was *vir justus et ten ex propositi,* and at the time of his death, he was the oldest Counsellor at the bar of the Supreme Court, in his native State, having seen all the eminent men, once associated with him, called to their rest.

He continued to reside in Somerville from 1819 until the spring of 1841, almost universally beloved. In the meantime he had been subjected to affliction in the death, first of his little children, and then of his beloved wife, on the first day of September, 1829. He had also, after mature reflection and from a deep sense of the importance of the step he was taking, in May, 1822, united with this church on confession of his faith. His parents were members, his wife was an earnest and a beautiful Christian, and he himself, after making his confession of faith ever afterwards adorned the doctrines which he professed by a pure and holy life, in which was abundantly manifested the power of piety and practical godliness. He was an Elder of this Church frequently, until he removed to Trenton. He had its welfare always in his heart. He represented it often in the General Synod. He was one of the committee appointed to the Synod in 1830, to revise the constitution of our church, and wrote the chapter on discipline, almost exactly as it was adopted. It is a fine exhibition of a broad and judicious legal mind, applying the great principles of justice and truth, in their connection with the proper discipline of the church, in language which is at once accurate, comprehensive and definite. There is really nothing equal to it in any other book of discipline that I am acquainted with.

During the discussions which ensued, preparatory to the adoption of this constitution, he was often brought into conflict in debate, with the Hon. Abraham Van Vechten, of Albany, and then we had the very finest possible display of forensic argument and logic. The result when reached, generally seemed to settle the question fully and forever, in the minds of those who had heard the profound arguments adduced on either side

During almost the whole period of his residence in Somerville, he was Superintendent of the Sabbath School, and gave his personal attendance to its exercises on the Sabbath day. This school was organized in 1816 on the the first Sabbath in April, by a few persons under the influence of Mrs. Rev. J. S. Vredenburgh, and was one of the first Sabbath Schools in the State of New Jersey. Two others it is understood were coeval with it ; one at New Brunswick, brought into existence through the agency of Mrs. J. R. Hardenburgh : and another at Elizabeth-town, by Mrs. Dr. McDowel. Our school has lived and flourished through all the intervening years, been a fountain of life to the Church, and ought to live in all coming time. The mode of conducting Sabbath schools, has greatly changed since the first efforts were made in those early days. To me it seems, that all the changes have not been for the better. When the pupils were taught the Catechisms, committed to memory and recited the Scriptures and so many of our beautiful hymns, I believe really that there was more important instruction imparted and more good done. I know at least, that many of our best, most useful and excellent members of the church, were trained up under Gov. Vroom and his associates. His heart was engaged deeply in this good work, and he has often said that he enjoyed it greatly. Some of his best and happiest hours were spent in it, and perhaps he did as much good in this humble way as in higher and more public employments.

When it became necessary, in 1834, to rebuild this Church—an enterprise which Gov. Vroom, with many others, believed to have been much too long postponed ; he became one of five men, who donated the largest sum that was given in aid of the work. Indeed, without these donations, it is hardly probable that the effort could have been made successful. It had often been attempted before, and finally gained the popular assent only through stress of circumstances. I remember well, how entirely his heart was in it, and how he rejoiced in the happy completion of the building in which we now worship.

Gov. Vroom continued to reside in Somerville until 1841, when, having resumed his practice at the Bar, and his business being principally in the Supreme Court at Trenton, convenience seemed to require a change. He left his place among us, but his heart continued with us still. He regarded this Church as *his* Church ; and always loved, when he could, to return here to be present at its Communion seasons. No one was ever more deeply interested in every thing having relation to its peace and prosperity, and no one rejoiced more when it seemed to be blessed and flourished. You remember how he came here at the Semi-Centenary of our County Bible Society, and made one of his

finest and most effective public addresses. It was the last
time his voice was heard among us, commending to his fellow citizens the scriptures, the religion of Christ which they
teach, and the necessity of practical godliness in life and in
death.

The last change which he made in the form of his life
while among us, was one of great importance to him, and
proved, I think, to be eminently proper and productive of
happiness. He contracted on the 4th of November, 1840,
a second marriage with Maria Matilda, the only daughter
of Gen. Wall, of Burlington. He was at the time a member of Congress. In the spring of the next year he fixed
his residence finally in Trenton. In that city he continued
to reside, with the exception of the four years which he
spent in Berlin, Prussia, until his death.

This seems the proper place to mention two great sorrows which fell upon our friend after he had removed from
us, in the death of his two sons. John died May 27th,
1865, in a most sudden and unexpected manner, sitting in
his father's office at Trenton. He was perhaps one of the
finest educated young lawyers at the bar of the State. After a full course at Rutgers' he studied law in his father's
office, and received license a few months before his father
was appointed to the Mission in Berlin. He went with
him there, and during the first winter attended a course of
lectures in the celebrated University in that city, in law
and philosophy. During the next summer he traveled extensively, and mostly on foot, through Germany, Switzerland
and Italy—remaining a long time in Rome, and studying

thoroughly its history, antiquities and art-collections. Then he spent the winter in Paris, and made himself master of the French language. With all these advantages he returned home to commence the practice of his profession in Jersey City. He had already gained a prominent place at the Bar, when death took him, and cut off suddenly all the budding hopes which seemed to promise so much fruit ! The affliction bowed his father down almost to the earth— "he mourned for him as for his first born."

Then came the death of Govie his youngest son, just after he had finished his collegiate course, when his father thought to make him his companion, and lean upon him in his old age, and have him attend to all his business which was becoming burdensome. Oh ! I remember well how he sorrowed under these bereavements. He seemed like good old Jacob, to be prepared to say, " I shall go down to the grave with my sons mourning." But like a Christian man, he justified God and waited in patience to see why he had been called to suffer so much in the destruction of his fondest hopes. That he ever saw how the loss could be made up to him, we cannot affirm, but that he waited patiently for the fulfillment of the promise, " all things shall work together for good," we have sufficient assurance, for he went on his way, trusting in God and believing that " what we know not now, we shall know hereafter ;" and thought most of "the loving kindness of the Lord "

We shall be obliged to return and to speak more fully of some of the circumstances alluded to in this brief way, in another connection, and therefore, proceed to delineate the character of our friend, because

"These are deeds that should not pass away,
And names that should not wither."

As a man we may say he had a presence that was impressive, and indicated to an intelligent observer the superior qualities which distinguished the individual. Perhaps it was true of him, as it was sometimes said, that the first sight seemed to give the idea of something stern and almost forbiding. He certainly was not a smiler or a flatterer: he did not try to insinuate himself into any one's confidence, and he never went about making friends, by seeming to be all things to all men. But alway when you came to know him, and had inspired his confidence or gained his esteem you found that there never was a kinder, a truer, or a nobler heart beating in any man's bosom. His friends were his friends always, unless they rudely or deceitfully forfeited his esteem ; and perhaps he lost as few of them as ever any man did. He certainly had as many who were willing to go with him to the end, as ever any man had. Around him gathered such a band of friends as the world knows but few, "the noblest names in the great host of truth's advancing ranks." I think it is true, that his friends not only grew in his esteem constantly, but that he held them every day by a firmer and stronger grasp. The nearer they came to his heart, the warmer they felt its pulsations to be, and the more they attached themselves to him, the more they saw how much he deserved it ! He was so honest, so unsophisticated, so magnanimous, so true, so willing to allow for human weakness, if he found that it carried with it a heart, that he did not need to lose his friends. He had faith in men, and cherished no morbid, misanthropic sentiments

He knew men, and seldom trusted where there was no integrity or self respect: or refused his confidence where there were qualities which gave proper security in its bestowal. His sense of honor, integrity and uprightness influenced him in everything. He would support his friend or defend his clients to the last ; but a miscreant, a scoundrel, or an acknowledged criminal, could find no help from him ! He was an example to be copied by men in the legal profession and on the bench, and if his upright, honorable and truthful course, was always followed, justice would be more rightly administered, property be more secure, and fraud and vice seldomer escape merited condemnation ! There is nothing that demoralizes a people so quickly, as through chicanery, technicality or bribery, to suffer the guilty to escape and justice to be defrauded of her proper reward.

Gov. Vroom was a gentleman—by nature and by feeling, as much as by breeding an te lucation ! He could not smile and smile and then act as a villain ; but his smile and his affability meant something It came from his feelings and his heart ! You might meet him in the street ten times in a day : you would always receive from him the recognition of a gentleman ! His port and bearing indicated his culture, and high breeding, and a child would receive the same respectful attention that he accorded to the highest in station and influence. Indeed children who knew him generally were attached to him, and among them he counted some of his dearest friends ! It was a sight calculated to do your heart good to see how he cherished them, and how confidingly they trusted and loved him ! When he was with them, he almost seemed to feel that he was himself again a child ; but he was yet, even when he had come down to their feelings and condition, a dignified gentleman ! Among strangers he was a marked man ! Every one who met him seemed to concede at once that he could not be an ordinary individual, and anxiously enquired who he was ! I have had occasion to see this in a great variety of instances both at home and in Europe. I have seen him among the highest bred society in both, and remarked how he always bore himself with proper dignity and urbanity, and received the deferential respect of all who knew or approached him. He seemed to command it ; and they felt that nothing was more proper than to concede it.

We must next consider him as a lawyer : and here it is pertinent to remark in the beginning, that his mind was of a superior cast and character—clear, logical and eminently perceptive ! He mastered a subject very soon, and when he came to discuss it, it was evident that he had seen it in all its important bearings. He could not therefore as an advocate be surprised or thrown off his guard, by arguments or views that were new to him, and that he was not prepared to meet ; and when he had discussed a case, there was never much to add, that could be said to be new or important to a proper comprehension of it. He had read law extensively and mastered the great principles on which it was founded.

Moreover the view which he had taken of it was, not only thorough but honest. He loved truth too much, and he always esteemed justice too highly to allow his mind to be unduly swayed by sympathy, or fatally influenced by any improper considerations. Few men at the Bar have exhibited uniformly, more solid judgment, more thorough integrity, and more firm adherence to principle, than he did. He was therefore a safe Counselior, and seldom left his client any reason to feel that all had not been done for him that could properly have been done.

As a speaker he was clear, logical, persuasive and earnest. There have been men who were more eloquent, and who had the power of moving and transporting their hearers more than he ever did ; but there have been only a few, who *uniformly* spoke more to the point, and held those to whom they were speaking more closely to the subject of argument, and more thoroughly informed their understanding. His voice had in it a soft sounding melody, his words were well chosen, and expressed clearly his meaning without any redundancy, and when his heart was engaged he became pathetic and moving. In fact he was uniformly heard with respect and attention, and often with the deepest interest and the most thorough conviction. He was a strong man in Court, and made for himself a reputation, as a barrister, which was both honorable and admirable. In after years he will be spoken of as one of the great lawyers, who have adorned the jurisprudence of our State, and left upon it the impress of their mind and character for the benefit and instruction of future times.

During the whole time he held the office of Governor of the State, he was also Chancellor, and decided a variety of important cases. Some of them which had a connection with Ecclesiastical affairs, were unusual, if not entirely new. His decisions have stood the test of time, and are quoted as law in all the Courts. It has been remarked by those whose opinions ought to be authority, that it has been found necessary to review fewer of his decisions, than those of almost any one of the Chancellors of the State. Those of Williamson and Green alone, I believe, are regarded as being of equal authority, on account of their learning and accuracy.

His messages and proclamations, as Governor, were always distinguished by one thing which is not common, but which certainly is of great importance in a Christian community and from a Christian Statesman. He uniformly acknowledged the existence of the Christian religion, the divine mission of the Lord Jesus Christ, with the benefit of public worship and the importance of the means of grace. I know of no one of our Governors who has made these recognitions so uniformly and distinctly, except Governor Olden. The most of the proclamations issued are merely the language of Deism, and could as well have been written by one of the Roman Emperors, or one of the Heathen Philosophers. This is not what a Christian people ought to receive, or what they have a right to expect, from one to whom they have entrusted executive functions. Gov Vroom was too much of a Christian Statesman to succumb to the demands of that morbid infidelity which exists but too fatally in the feelings of many of our public men. He respected himself, and the Christian sentiment of the best of our citizens too much, to perpetuate any such folly.—

Gov. Vroom must be considered as one of the ablest men of the New Jersey Bar. He argued during his practice, almost all the great cases which were in litigation. He argued them well. He did not always carry his case successfully through and obtain a judgment in his favor ; but his client never found any reason to say, that he had neglected the interest committed to his care, or that he had not done all that learning and energy could have done to secure success. He no doubt had a proper sense of the value of his services, but he never oppressed his client by excessive charges. I think it is true, that none of the eminent lawyers of our State have labored so earnestly and so successfully for such a moderate compensation. He felt his responsibility and never refused his counsel and assistance to a poor man, because he knew that he was not able properly to remunerate his service. He was never made rich by his profession and practice, and he did a vast amount of work for which he received but little if any compensation. He was a benefactor often, instead of being himself benefited by his efforts ; and the blessing of those whom he had counselled and defended came abundantly upon him.

Gov. Vroom was also a statesman and politician. He did not enter early into the arena of public life. The views which he had probab'y imbibed were in obeyance when he came upon the stage ; and the political organization, if there ever was one with which he would naturally have affiliated; had become demoralized and almost extinct. But the time came which opened before him a field of action, and he entered upon it with ardor. Gen. Jackson offered the members of the old Federal party, an opportunity of uniting with his personal friends in advancing him to office, and they almost unanimously embraced it. With this party, in all its varying fortunes and successes, he continued to associate unto the last. He was never a violent politician, but he was an earnest one, just as in everything else he was earnest, when he was convinced of the right and proposed to himself proper ends and action.

His statesmanship was intelligently liberal and enlarged : and I believe, uniformly sought the public good more than party ends or personal ambition   If he had been more subservient, he might have been more successful ; but the truth is, he was not intended for a successful politician. His knees were not supple enough, his character not sufficiently selfish, and he could not do what his conscience and conviction of right, taught him that he ought not to do.   There were times when a little yielding, a little personal subserviency to men in power, an implied promise to be what he knew they wanted him to be, would have carried him into high places.   But he never could be induced to sell himself for place or promotion.   The offices which he filled sought him, instead of his seeking the office.   His friends made him what he was, but he never solicited advancement from any one.

But the crowning beauty and excellency of Gov. Vroom's character, remains yet to be presented—he was a Christian lawyer and statesman.   Not a Christian man only, but a man who carried his Christianity into every position which he ever filled.   He was not ashamed of Christ, or of the faith which he had professed in Christ, as being "the only name given under heaven by which a sinner can be saved." His christianity was deeply seated in his heart, and went with him wherever he went, and influenced him in his daily conduct and life. It had loving power in his soul and made him a devotional man. He worshiped God in his house ; and I remember, when he had been absent at Trenton, as Governor of the State, how happy he seemed to be, when having returned home and Saturday evening, he joined in our weekly prayer meeting. He would seem to pour his whole heart out in his prayers and the pathos of his utterance often bathed the whole assembly in tears. His supplications were so earnest, so humble, so childlike, so pleading, as if he felt, "I will not let Thee go, except thou bless me."

Before I came to live in Somerville, I was told by a plain man from the country, with great wonderment and admiration, how he came to his house in the village here quite early in the morning, and was kept waiting half an hour in the office, while he was reading the scriptures and praying with his family. The man seemed unable to understand how it was possible, that the Governor of the State of New Jersey, could do such a thing. He thought that men in high places were always worldly and ungodly men ; and then said the man, "he prayed so ; he made me feel as I had never felt before. Oh ! I never expected to hear such a thing."

While I was with him in Berlin, he sought from Baron Humbolt the privilege of an introduction for me. The Baron very freely accorded the request, and appointed the

day and hour for it to take place. We attended, and were
ushered into his study. When the introduction had taken
place, and we were seated, he commenced a very rapid and
animated conversation : asking various questions, and gain-
ing the information he supposed we could give. This continued several minutes, when he seemed to recollect, that I
had scarcely entered into the conversation at all ; and to
afford him an opportunity of a personal talk with me, he
called Mr. Vroom's attention to a picture hanging some distance from us. When he had risen and gone to view it,
the Baron turned to me, and in an undertone said, " we
admire your friend here very much : he has obtained more
influence with the Government here, than almost any other
Ambassador ever sent to us from the United States. He is
a very judicious and excellent man ; but isn't he a little
queer ? I asked how ? Why there are so many things he
won't do, and he don't attend any of our dances and never
goes to the theatre." I said Mr. Vroom is a practical Christian : a pious, godly man. He looked at me with an expression of countenance, in which there was a good deal of
surprise and a lurking smile of mirth, and said, "Yes that is
it ; Yes that must be it ;" and this settled the question in
the Baron's mind. Mr. Vroom was a *Pietist*; one of those
good people, of whom the Baron had heard, and some of
whom he had probably seen ; *good people*, but they know
nothing about philosophy. Humboldt himself had no idea
of religion ; he did not even believe in a personal divinity.
His God was the spirit of nature. No wonder he thought
Gov. Vroom a little queer.

The Christianity of Mr. Vroom was built upon, and grew out of the doctrines of our Church. He understood the faith of his own Church fully. He had studied it, and experienced its power in his heart. He was a Calvinist from knowledge, conviction and experience. He was nothing else, and he tolerated nothing else. He traced this form of faith, back through Calvin and Augustine, to St. Paul. He knew that as often as this faith had been lost to the Church : the power of Christian life had departed with it ; and that it always came back in seasons of special divine influence. His piety was therefore the scriptural piety—"Christ in us the hope of glory." It was not in name, in rites, in sacraments, in forms, but in the *power of a new life :* and because this life was in him, he daily lived with God. The Bible was his constant companion, and prayer like his daily food. I remember his showing me once, a small Testament, much worn and full of marked texts ; and his remarking how he had carried it with him for many years wherever he went ; and then he pointed out some of the texts with the initials of the preacher and the date, and remarked how much he valued it, because it enabled him to recall so many excellent sermoms, and Sabbaths which had been very impressive and precious to him. A year or two afterwards, in the same place, he told me that he had lost this little book, and how he grieved over the misfortune. It was a memorial of his religious thought and experience, extending through many important years of his life, and as such almost invaluable. The circumstance shows how much he had reflected on the great subject of religion and how precious the enjoyments of it were to him, and how much he was interested in preserving this little memorial of his past experience and pleasure.

At this period of his life, he was frequently called to speak at religious anniversaries. Such as the Bible Society, the Tract Society and the American Colonization Society. When the first company of Missionaries from our Church, went out to Borneo, he delivered a very beautiful and interesting farewell address to them, in the Old Middle Church in New York City. He was then, and continued to be for many years afterwards, one of the Presidential Committee of the American Board of Commissioners for Foreign Missions ; and he was a Vice President of the American Bible and Colonization Societies at the time of his death.

As a Christian man, he was a man of large views and generous impulses, and he cherished a zealous and earnest spirit. He gave to religious objects abundantly, and he rejoiced always to know that practical Christianity was anywhere advancing. Nothing could have ever made him a bigot, or confined his sympathies or charities to sectionalism. It was the kingdom of Christ that he tried to build up, and not any party, or the views of any party in it, though he loved most his own church.

His nervous depressions had nothing to do with his piety. Their origin was a physical one ; and the proper treatment was medicinal. He was subject to them as long as I knew him : and I remember more than one severe and acute attack. His last sickness commenced in one of those depressions. I had never before seen him so despondent and so gloomy. But after a few days it passed away. The cloud was lifted, and the light shone out through it, and then his face became as luminous as an angel's, and he went to Heaven Elijah like on " the chariots of salvation." His only anxiety was soon to go, and his prayer, " now letest thou thy servant depart in peace, for mine eyes have seen thy salvation." It was at *home*, at *home* that he longed most to be, and his last words were, " I am going home this morning." A great and a good man is lost to this Church and to the world : but his memory will long be fondly cherished by many. I hope to make it one of the treasured gems of this Christian household which he loved so much, and in the communion of which he lived so long and died. I count it one of my chiefest honors that I obtained his confidence and his friendship, and retained them to the last ; and that I am permitted to twine this chaplet of pale, sad autumn flowers and lay it on his grave. It is but little, when I consider what he was to me, and what I owe him, for his council and advice on many deeply interesting and trying occasions. I have had many friends, and owe them many things, but I have found no other friend altogether like him. His death closes up a host of pleasant memories, and seems to leave me almost alone But I am glad that he lived so nobly, and that he died so sweetly. The thought of it is like the incense of a rich perfume, and the memory of it will be cherished as encouragement and strength, with which to be armed when for me the great conflict comes. It is not— " No, not death to die in such repose and confidence." Remember, says one, that some of the brightest drops in the

chalice of life may still remain for us in old age. The last
draught which a kind Providence gives us to drink, though
near the bottom of the cup, may have at that very bottom,
instead of dregs, most costly pearls," and so it was in this
case. He probably never had such adoring views of Christ
and of Heaven, as on his death bed when his face shone as
if the light of glory was already beaming upon it.

The public services which Gov. Vroom rendered were
numerous, and some of them very important. At an early
age, while yet a resident at Flemington, he was appointed
Deputy Attorney General of the State of New Jersey.
This appointment was unquestionably an act of friendship,
but it was well and worthily bestowed. It had no political
significance. His father was a Federalist and supported
Washington and Hamilton in the peculiar policy which they
adopted and endeavored to enforce, after the Federal Constitution had been formed and accepted by the States. It is
probable that the son sympathized with the same views, but
there is nothing to show what his sentiments on the political questions of the day really were. In the year 1824,
however, he assumed a definite position and advocated the
election of Andrew Jackson, for President. Before this time
the Federal party had, in effect, been disbanded and ceased
to exist. John Quincy Adams went over and joined the
party of Mr. Jefferson, and was supported for the Presi-
dency by them. The old Federalists felt indignant at his
desertion of his father's friends, and as a matter of course,
united with those who were opposed to him. In this course
of action Mr. Vroom was followed and supported by a most

all the prominent Federalists in Somerset County. He was soon called into public life, by being elected a member of the Assembly in 1826 and 1827, and again in 1829. In that year his party being largely in the ascendant, and the election of Chief Magistrate belonging to the Legislature in *joint meeting*, he was chosen Governor and Chancellor of the State, in the place of Isaac H. Williamson, who had been an incumbent of that office for many previous years. He was re-elected in 1830 and 1831. In 1832 Samuel L. Southard superceded him : but *he* having secured his election as a Senator of the United States, the Governor's office devolved upon Mr. Seeley In 1835 Mr. Vroom was again appointed Governor, and re-elected in 1834 and 1835. In 1836 he declined the appointment on account of impaired health. He was confined to his house all that winter by his constitutional disease. During this year he went by appointment of the President, Martin Van Buren, with Nicholas Vans Murray of Maryland, and Thomas Mann Randolph of Virginia, to adjust the claims of the Choctaw Indians, in the State of Mississippi. Returning home during the summer, the Commission met again in the next autumn, and finally adjourned to the city of Washington, where they made up and submitted their report, and it was adopted by Congress. In the Autumn of 1839 he was elected to Congress This gave rise to *the Broad Seal Controversy*. Gov. Pennington gave the certificate of election to the members on the opposition ticket ; but the returns upon which he based his action, were short by omitting the votes of the townships of Millville, in Cumberland County, and South Amboy, in Middlesex County. This fact was certified to by the Secretary of State ; and armed with his certificate, Gov. Vroom and his associates went to Washington, took their seats in the House of Representatives, and maintained their position. It was said at the time, that his argument before the Committee of Investigation appointed by the House was one of the ablest and most conclusive arguments which he ever made. He served out his term ; but in 1841 was swept under by the tide raised by " Log Cabins."

He had in the mean time taken up his permanent residence in Trenton. In 1844 he was elected by his friends in Somerset, as one of their delegates to the Constitutional Convention. He received the appointment of Chairman of the Committee on the Legislative department, and reported the article, defining the powers of the Legislature, as it was adopted, and remains in the Constitution of the State at the present time.

In 1852 he was chosen one of the Electors for President and Vice President, and gave his vote for Franklin Pierce. In 1853 Gov. Fort nominated him for the office of Chief Justice of the Supreme Court ; but he at once, on the day on which it was received, declined the appointment. In mid-summer of the same year, he received from the President the nomination as United States Minister to Prussia. He was tendered a public dinner by his friends, as an expression of their sentiments for the honor done him, and their appreciation of his character. He sailed with his whole family soon after for Europe, and resided four years in Berlin.

In 1857 after Mr. Buchanan had been elected President, he requested to be relieved from his position and trust, and returned to Trenton, to resume his place at the Bar once more. While in Prussia he negotiated treaties of Commerce and Amity with Baden, and some of the other minor German Principalities, which settled, specifically the status of persons who had emigrated, and after becoming citizens of the United States, had returned to their native land. His residence abroad afforded him a source of pleasure in reflection during the remainder of his life. It had greatly enlarged his knowledge. and perfected his views of many things, only understood by seeing and knowing them as they are.

In 1861, he was appointed a member of the Peace Convention, which assembled in Washington, before hostilities had actually commenced. He was one of the members of the Committee on the State of the Union, of which Mr. Guthrie of Kentucky, was chairman. He labored earnestly to prevent the impending conflict ; and I know he never regret ed his efforts in that direction, but only that they had not succeeded.

At the close of the war, he was appointed, with Gov. Olden, a Commissioner of the Sinking Fund. The public does not know yet, and possibly may never fully know, what they owe to these two pure, high minded and honorable men, for the integrity and wisdom with which they have managed this important trust. If their views and principles are carried out. in about ten years the war debt of the State will have been liquidated. But it is feared, that sel-

fish men in the future Legislatures, may interfere and try
to grasp what has been with so much care accumulated.
Attempts have already been made, but so far fortunately
without success.

Gov. Vroom was appointed one of the Electors again in
1868, and gave his vote for Horatio Seymour, of the State
of New York, for President. He succeeded to the office of
Reporter to the Supreme Court, on the death of his son
John, and published six volumes of reports.

In 1837 he was honored with a degree, creating him a
Doctor of Laws, from Columbia College, and again from
Princeton in 1857. He was a Trustee of Rutgers' College
from 1828, and at the time of his death the oldest member
of the Board. Thus you perceive, that like the eminent
men referred to in our text, after a busy and honorable life,
he died in a good old age, full of years and full of honors

His life was indeed an active one ; and when we look over
the catalogue of the public trusts conferred on him, it
may be said that he was as frequently honored as any man
from our little State has ever been ; and in every one of
his offices he was useful, successful and honorable. He has
transmitted a perfectly unspotted reputation to his children.
No one ever dared to insinuate that he was not always, and
in all circumstances and times, an honorable and pure
minded man. They might dissent from his views, and
other men as good as he, differed with him in politics, but
they did not dare to impeach the integrity of his character :
and this is where the high honor which we claim for him, is
made most evident and conspicuous. Contrast him with

other men in public life ; how fair and bright his fame is. How much we need such men ! How much society and the public welfare have suffered in his death ! Honesty and honor seem almost to have become rare and unfrequent virtues among men in high places. There are a precious few who are not defiled, or at least accused of defilement.

Gov. Vroom, notwithstanding his constitutional tendency to a certain form of disease, enjoyed a large portion of good health, an l lived beyond four score years, and he preserved his mental vigor, with his memory and perceptive faculties, until the very last. You could not perceive that in mind he was an old man. He felt his age and spoke of it often, but when he came to converse or to act, he was young after all. Only a short while previous to his decease, he went into the Court of Errors, and astonished the Judges and the bar by the vigor of his argument, and the profundity and learning with which he illustrated and enforced it. He was himself again, and held his auditors in profound attention for two hours.

His old age was perfectly beautiful. He could be found in his office every day. He had always something to do. He was in possession of a competence. He was happy in his domestic relations. He was contented with the honors and distinctions to which he had attained. He had early attended to " the one thing needful." He was not afraid to die, and cherished a good hope of eternal life through Jesus Christ the Saviour of men; and he waited calmly and hopefully, " the days of his appointed time, until his change should come " He had lived long, lived well, and departed hoping to live eternally in Heaven. In thinking of it, I have realized, what has been so beautifully said by another : " Death is the justification of all the ways of the Christian, the last end of all his sacrifices—that touch of the great master which completes the picture." "At eventide—says the holy word, there shall be light."

He ought to be held up as an eminent and important example to men in the legal profession. His life proves that it is possible that there should be a Christian lawyer, and also that he should be a successful one. Gov. Vroom, and others like him and coeval with him, have indeed proved this important fact most unequivocally. It ought to be considered by young men, when entering upon their life course. Integrity and uprightness are the safest and most successful. Honorable dealings stand a man in good stead always ; and the true path to happiness and success, is in knowing the truth, doing the truth, and living the truth. A correspondence fixed with Heaven is always a sure and noble anchor.

There are ways of becoming rich very fast ; and men have managed to mount up rapidly into places of profit and trust ; but there are those who have fallen down and become poor as rapidly as they mounted upwards. Ill-gotten gain is an uncertain possession ; and even when a man holds it until he dies, and transmits it to his children, he cannot always transmit a blessing with it. In not a few instances, it proves itself to have been only a curse. Greedy grasping, and avaricious over-reaching are never safe. Providence never smiles on such a course, and the possession of dishonest gain is never a real blessing. It does not bring men to honor but to disgrace.

But the crowning glory of Gov. Vroom's life was its Godliness. He was a true Christian, he was a Christian always : and was never anywhere anything that a Christian may not be. His Conversion was a decided spiritual change. It realized the inspired definition of practical Christianity— "Christ in you the hope of glory." It made him a spiritually minded and a devotional man. His piety was a great power, living in him and working in him daily. It taught him every day ta realize, that " we live and move and have our being in God ; and that he is never far from us." He carried his conscientiousness with him, into all the active affairs of life for half a century and more. He could be nothing else but decided in his religious views and opinions. He knew in whom he had believed. He had been taught what the fruits of faith are, and ught to be—that they are not in *name*, but in *power*. No wonder he died so calmly and so sweetly, with the word " HOME" lingering on his lips— " I am going home"—" I want every one to know how precious Jesus has been to me." The salvation which Jesus has wrought out for his people, was the hope of his salvation ; and the *home* to which he knew that he was certainly going, was " the mansions in the Father's house." which Jesus went before us to prepare, " that where he is, his children may all likewise be."—be there with him. Home and rest, in God and in love ; deep repose in that still country, where the mystery of life is solved, and the most feverish heart lays down its load at last.

> " His soul, enlarged from its vile bonds has gone
> To that REFULGENT world where it shall swim
> In liquid light and float on seas of bliss."

No wonder some men could not understand him—thought
him singular, and unnecessarily precise in his life and conduct. It is a *strait way* in which we are walking onward to
God. It will not allow of everything ; nor can we be everything, and carry everything with us. Sir Walter Raleigh
has well said,

> " Or death and judgment, Heaven and Hell
> Who oft doth think, must needs die well,"

and *this*,—is it not the great end of living—living to die
well ? Is any life a successful one, if it does not end well ?
There is advancement not only but there is also joy in a
translation to a higher life.

> " Thou takest not away O, death,
> Thou strikest—absence perisheth—
>   Indifference is no more !
> The future brightens on the sight ;
> For on the past has fallen a light,
>   That tempts us to adore."

Such a beautiful ending of life, how attractive it is ! Every
duty well done, every important interest well secured and
every responsibility fairly and fully met ; honored by men,
approved by Heaven and waiting only for the summons to
come up higher and enter upon the nobler life ! It seems
to complete and satisfy the demands of reason, conscience
and faith, and must be approved of God.

It is what we would desire for ourselves, and what we pray may be the end of the pilgrimage of every one who seeks to " serve God in sincerity and in truth." Indeed, it is what is promised in the Holy Scriptures, and what God's people often attain to. " Now letest thou thy servant depart in peace, for mine eyes have seen thy salvation." When it comes we say,

> " He rests. as sets the morning star, which goes
> Not down behind the darkened west, nor hides
> Obscured amid the tempests of the sky—
> But swells away into the light of Heaven."

TRIBUTES OF RESPECT.

THE DEATH.

[Extract from the State Gazette, of Nov. 19, 1873.]

A long and useful life, an honorable and unblemished career, were closed yesterday by the death of Gov. Peter D. Vroom. The oldest counsellor at the Bar of New Jersey, having practiced over fifty years, and widely known, not only by his professional connections, but by his social intercourse, the intelligence of his death will awaken personal regrets in every part of the State. Gov. Vroom had been confined to his bed about a fortnight. Previous to that time he had shown an activity of mind and an industry remarkable for his years. He suffered, we believe, from no ailment save that which is beyond human skill,—old age and the exhaustion which it brings. Having lived a life beautiful in its purity and its usefulness, exemplary in its social virtues and its professional excellence, having been faithful to every public trust and an ornament to the profession of which he was a member, he has died a death, surrounded by his family, which, unaccompanied by pain, was beautiful in its serenity and peace.

The best eulogy that can be given of the deceased is a simple account of his private life and public services.

THE OBSEQUIES.

Yesterday morning was like a Sabbath. The air was keen and cold, and silence reigned. The flag on the State House floated at half-mast, and the business marts were closed. The leading men of the State were seen wending their way to the family mansion of the Vrooms, to take part in the last ceremony of parting with the remains of one whose name had become a household word, and whose death was a fitting close to a well spent and studious life.

In a chamber of the mansion lay all that was mortal of ex-Gov. Vroom. He looked natural. The body was neatly attired, and the countenance was calm, and bore the appearance of a peaceful sleep. The inscription on the coffin-lid was :

PETER D. VROOM,

Dec. 12th, 1791.

DIED, Nov. 18th, 1873.

The coffin was covered with black cloth, and on the lid were wreaths of flowers. In the family home with the crowd of guests there was stillness befitting such an occasion as the passing away of the master. The Bench and Bar of the State, amongst the guests, were fully represented. Eighty-two years in a young nation—what a life ! Born in the infant days of the new government, familiar from boyhood with facts that have become history, in the latter years of his life Peter D. Vroom was an authority of precedent, which, after all, is the wisdom of the world and the foundation of what we know. And as we take the last farewell of one we have known so long, in the silence, fancy connected the past with the present, and we said with Der-shanoff, the Russian poet, for the translation of which we are indebted to Sir John Bowring :

" Thou the beginning with the end hast bound
And beautifully mingled life with death. "

Filing in came the principal citizens of the State ; men famous in law, learning and literature ; men who have stood in battle array when the destinies of the nation were at stake ; men who have in private walks of life adorned the character of citizens, and who, in the last scene paid homage to the worth of the departed.

And while the chambers were filled with the best citizens, in the hush and calm of the household, where Death reigned, there arose the voice of prayer from the pastor of the First Presbyterian Church, the Rev. Dr. Hall.

His prayer was the voice of praise and resignation ; praise that the departed had lived so good and valuable a life as an example to his fellow men, and also that he had nobly and honorably maintained the duty of a Christian. God was thanked for the circumstances in which they met that day. They had no right to bring complainings into the presence of the good Father, but rather to be thankful that the departed had lived so long to bear testimony to the truth. What had not God done for him in his long life ? It had enabled him for so many years to show forth his faith in Christ and to be a pillar in his Church, and to be an example to all around him. And for that they would come with praise instead of lamentations, and ask that they might be blessed and profited by the example of the life which had so honorably closed. He asked that the life and death might be sanctified to all, that they might be enabled to lead good lives, and at the close of life triumph in death through Jesus Christ. The praise was closed with the Lord's prayer and the Benediction.

The coffin was then taken to the hearse by the carriers, who were Titus H. Stout, James Hammell, Joshua S. Day, Charles Biles, J. J. Johnson, Benjamin S. Disbrow.

The cortege proceeding immediately to the depot, taking the 11 o'clock train to Somerville, Gov. Parker, the Secretary of State, and other State officials, the members of the Supreme Court and Court of Errors and Appeals, the Mercer county courts, delegations from the State bar and bar of Mercer county, including the Chancellor and Attorney General, and the Mayor and officers of the city of Trenton accompanied the remains. All the State offices were closed, the flags on the Capitol and City Hall were at half-mast, the Court of Errors had adjourned until Monday, the Mercer county courts for one week, and Mayor Briest of Trenton had issued proclamation desiring that stores along the route of the procession should be closed from 9 until 11, A. M. Such respect has not been shown to any one in New Jersey since the death of Hon. Wm. L. Dayton, Minister to France.

The pall bearers were ex-Chancellor Green, ex-Gov. Olden, Chief Justice Beasley, Gov Parker, Attorney-General

Gilchrist, Abraham Browning, Cortlandt Parker, and Judge Scudder.

The remains, on arriving at Somerville, were taken to the First Reformed Dutch Church,and a sermon suitable to the occasion preached by Rev. Dr. Messler, the pastor. In the pulpit besides the preacher, were Dr. Hall, of Trenton, and and Rev. John P. Knox, of Newton, Long Island.

The following gentlemen acted as pall bearers in Somerville, viz : R. H. Veghte, Caleb Miller, N. V. Steele, H. H. Garretson, P. A. Dumont, A J. Quick.

After the services in the Church were completed in the presence of a large concourse of people, the mortal remains were conveyed to the Dumont Cemetery on the south side of the Raritan river, where his former wife, his son John, and five of his little children rest.

It was a most impressive scene throughout, manifesting the firm attachments of his oldest and best friends, for one whom they had long known and honored. He had always shown a deep interest in the welfare of Somerville, and many tears demonstrated how sincerely it was reciprocated.

PEACE CONVENTION.

We add here a narrative of his services in the Peace Convention, in the city of Washington, in 1861. When the prospect of civil war had become threatening, and a convention representing the States, was held at Washington, to adopt some suitable basis of adjustment, Mr. Vroom was among the nine gentlemen appointed to represent New Jersey. He was a member of the committee composed of one from each State, to whom was referred the resolutions from New Jersey and the other States represented. In a letter written by one of the Commissioners, the labors of Gov. Vroom are spoken of in high terms. He was punctual and faithful, and in all consultations, says the writer, "We found him ever, and eminently calm, sagacious, and " his colleagues naturally and justly regarded him as the Nestor of the delegation, both as regards age and wisdom. In an address to the people of New Jersey, published in 1862, Gov. Vroom explained the causes which led to the failure of all propositions for peace, and disclosed the grounds upon which he and those who agreed with him thought it their duty to oppose the measures of the Lincoln administration. He emphatically disclaimed any concurrence in the doctrine of secession, declaring it to be a political heresy, but he insisted that the only legitimate object of the war was, as Congress had resolved, to suppress rebellion, establish the authority of the Constitution and restore the Union, and that this being accomplished, it should cease. And what was far more important even than this, the Constitution was disregarded and treated as if no longer binding, as an illustration of which the suspension by the President of the great writ of *habeas corpus* was referred to. At a latter period Gov. Vroom rendered important service by going to Somerset county when, during the war, excitement ran high and resistance to the draft was threatened, and delivering an address in which he counseled peaceful submission to the laws. This speech was always regarded as distinguished for force and eloquence. After referring to the right of free

discussion, and speaking of the war as a calamity to be deplored, he asked —" What then are we to do, in the situation in which we find ourselves placed. Let us resolve that this country, in its whole length and breadth is our country, and that we will save it if we can.   *   *   *   *
We must abide by the laws when duly made ; this has always been a principle of the Democratic creed, and I address myself to a law-loving people. We are not called upon to play the hypocrite and sing the praises of impolitic and bad laws, but we are to abide by them while they are laws. We may believe them to be unjust and unconditional, but in regard to their constitutionality we are not the judges. We are the people upon whom they are to operate, and who are to obey them. A judiciary has been provided to determine their constitutionality ; and that is our protection—it is the constitutional shield thrown around our rights." The success of Gov. Vroom in calming, with these words, an excited people, proved his power as a public speaker and the confidence and esteem with which he was regarded by the people of his native county after years of separation from them

Mr. Vroom labored earnestly in support of Gen. McClellan in 1864. and in 1868 was chosen one of the Presidential Electors and aided in casting the vote of the State for Horatio Seymour. In the later years of his life he accepted upon the death of his eldest son. who was Supreme Court reporter. that position, and the six volumes prepared by him attest the fidelity and the industry. characteristic of his entire life. with which he performed the duties of the office in his declining years. Upon the creation of the State Sinking Fund, Gov. Vroom was appointed one of the Commissioners, and until within a few days before he was stricken with the illness which has terminated his useful life, he gave his personal attention to the duties of this office, exhibiting a scrupulous and conscientious regard for all the transactions in which the interests of the State and the investment of her moneys were concerned.

In domestic and social life Gov. Vroom enjoyed the love and veneration of his immediate connections, and of all with whom he had intercourse. He was a member of the Dutch Reformed Church, a trustee of Rutgers' College, Vice President of the American Colonization and Bible Societies, and in 1857 the College of New Jersey conferred on him the degree of L. L. D. Retaining his faculties in a remarkable degree in his age, he did not cease his public labors until his energies gave way beneath the weight of accumulated years, and he may be said to have died, as he lived, in the service of his native State which he loved so well. Full of years and full of honors, Peter D. Vroom goes to his resting place, leaving behind him that which is more precious than " storied urn or animated bust "—a memory which those near to him and the citizens of his State must alike cherish and venerate.

RESOLUTIONS OF THE A. B SOCIETY.

The following preamble and memorial were adopted by the Board of Managers of the American Bible Society, at their meeting held December 4, 1873.

WHEREAS, It has pleased Almighty God to remove from among us by death the Hon. Peter D. Vroom, one of the Vice Presidents of this Society, the Board would pay a just tribute of respect to their lamented associate, and gratify their own feelings, by entering upon their minutes the following memorial.

Mr. Vroom was a warm friend of the Bible Society, and was elected Vice President in 1839, and with one exception was the oldest Vice President on our list. He died at his late residence in Trenton, N. J., in the eighty-second year of his age. He was the son of a revolutionary officer, and a native of Somerset County, N. J. He graduated at Columbia College in this city, at the early age of seventeen. He entered upon the profession of the law in 1813, and soon rose to eminence at the bar of his native State.

He was elected Governor of the State of New Jersey in 1829, and re-elected annually with the interval of a single term until the year 1836, when he declined the office. From 1838 to 1840, he was a member of Congress. He declined the office of Chief Justice of the State, and the same year went to Berlin as Minister Plenipotentiary of the United States at the court of Prussia, where he remained until 1857. In all public stations Governor Vroom served his State and the country at large with pre-eminent ability and with exemplary purity and elevation of character. Early in life he gave his heart to Christ, and united himself to the Reformed Church, which ever honored him as one of its wisest and most devoted friends.

His piety was simple but decided, and threw a charm over his intercourse with his fellow men which bound all hearts to him. In the fulness of a good old age, lamented and beloved by all who knew him, having served his generation, by the will of God, he has fallen on sleep. " The memory of the just is blessed."

ACTION OF THE SOMERSET COUNTY BAR.

At a meeting of the Somerset County Bar, at the recent session of the Court, the following action was taken in reference to the death of Hon. Peter D. Vroom :

IN MEMORIAM.

On Saturday, the 3d inst., the death of the Hon. Peter D. Vroom was announced by I. N. Dilts, Esq., whereupon His Honor, Judge Dalrymple, remarked :

That he thought it highly fitting that some notice should be taken at this time and place of the circumstance to which attention had been called. Gov. Vroom was a native of this county, and although, for a number of years, he had resided in Trenton, his affections had always centred upon the place of his birth, where he had retained a *quasi* residence—had kept up his church connections and relations of friendship with its citizens.

He was a great and good man. At the bar—in official positions in this State—in the National Councils, and at the Foreign Court where he represented our country, he was not only eminently popular, but ever fulfilled the duties devolved upon him in a manner unsurpassed by any of his contemporaries. And after having acted well his part in all the varied occupations of a long and useful life, he was—at his own request—brought to this, his native place for interment.

Among the evidences of the confidence placed in him by the people of this county, it is especially worthy of remark, that, although for more than six years a resident of Trenton, he was elected a representative of Somerset county in the convention which formed our present Constitution. When such a man dies, it is meet that his survivors should indicate the feelings excited by the event. The Court will gladly join with the Bar in placing upon record some memorial of our appreciation of his worth, and respect for his memory. For this purpose the Court now stan ls adjourned.

The Court having adjourned, on motion of H. M. Gaston, Esq., the Bar organized themselves by appointing His Honor Chairman. and J. D. Bartine, Secretary.

I. N. Dilts in moving the appointment of a committee to draft resolutions, expressive of the sense of the meeting, said :

In conformity with the sense of the Court as just expressed, and that of the bar here assembled, I rise to move the appointment of a committee to prepare resolutions expressing our appreciation of the character and worth of Gov. Vroom, and of respect for his memory. It would not become me on this occasion to attempt a biographical notice of the illustrious deceased, or a rehearsal of his many and valuable public services. That labor of love has already been in part performed, and doubtless will hereafter be completed by abler and more fitting hands But the bar of this county have been unwilling that one, who in past yea s shed so much lustre upon its history should pass away, without receiving fr m it some, however imperfect, notice.

Gov. Vroom was a native of this county of Somerset—a county which h is, perhaps, given to the State and country

more men who have attained to eminence in the various
walks of life, than any other like district in the State—possibly in the country. On the catalogue of her worthy sons,
stand enrolled the names of the Stocktons, the Frelinghuysens, the Southards, the Daytons,—and among them the
name of Peter D. Vroom occupies a rank second to none.

All the present members of this bar were so far removed
from Gov. Vroom in age as well as professional standing,
that we none of us, perhaps, enjoyed that intimacy with
him, to which his associates of more nearly equal position
were admitted. Still he was by no means an uninterested
observer of the efforts of the younger and rising members
of the legal profession. The words of friendly encouragement, as well as wise counsel, which fell from his, lips are
remembered by many.

Although not obtrusive or demonstrative, his attachments were strong and enduring. A friend once adopted
into that sacred relationship, was adopted for all time.
And no acquaintaince he was ever ready to manifest those
sweet charities which constitute the charm of life. But I
must forbear, as I do not design to estimate his career and
character, or to pronounce his eulogy. I simply add what
was said of another great light in the legal firmament,
"His private life was as beautiful, as his public course was
brilliant."

I move, sir, the appointment of a committee of three to
prepare resolutions expressive of the sense of this meeting,
on the decease of Gov. Vroom.

I. N. Dilts, H. M. Gaston, and J. V. Voorhees were ap-

TRIBUTES OF RESPECT. 59

pointed a committee, and reported the following resolutions :

WHEREAS, Hon. Peter D. Vroom, formerly and for a long time a member of the bar of this county, has departed this life since the last term of this Court : as some slight indication of our appreciation of the character and worth of the illustrious deceased :

Resolved, That in the death of the late ex-Gov. Peter D. Vroom, we unite with the bar of the State, in deploring the loss of an estimable citizen,—an able, learned and conscientious lawyer, an upright and laborious magistrate and judge, an exemplary and consistent Christian gentleman.

Resolved, That we recall with interest and reverence the virtues and graces that adorned his character the suavity and dignity which marked his intercourse with his professional brethren as well as the world—the vast erudition which eminently fitted him for the most exalted civil positions,—and the unspotted integrity which shone so brightly in his walk and conversation, as to shield him from even the assaults of temptation.

Resolved, That with pride we enroll his name high on the list of distinguished jurists and statesmen, given to our State and country by the county of Somerset, their common birth place.

Resolved, That we tender to his family our sincere condolence in their and our bereavement.

Resolved, That the Circuit Court of this county be requested to have a copy of these resolutions entered on the minutes, in testimony of respect for the memory of the deceased.

Mr. Bartine, in seconding the resolutions said :

I feel that it is proper for me as a member of this bar to add a few words in support of the resolutions offered by the committee.

Gov. Vroom was born, reared and educated in this County. He practiced at this bar for more than twenty years : and although absent for a long time his attachments to his native County remained strong and deep to the last, and having finished a long and useful life, his remains at his request were brought here and interred near the home of his childhood, on the banks of the Raritan.

It is fitting therefore, that this bar should in this manner

express the esteem in which it held his life, his character
and his public services, and have the same entered upon the
minutes of this Court.

It is unnecessary for me to say that he deserves this mark
of our respect. He adorned and exalted the profession of
law, and has left behind him an honored and venerated
name.

Few men of our State, if any, have so deservedly maintained for so long a period, an equal degree of intellectual
and moral distinction. His fame is secure. Nothing that
I may say can add to it. He was not only *great* but *good*. He
planted his standard firmly on the rock of virtue—the sum-
mit of human greatness, and upon his long record rests not
a single stain. He has done enough and done it so well and
so honorably as to entitle him to a front rank among the
great men of our State.

And beyond all this he died as he had lived, in the faith
of a Christian, adding another to the list of great men who
have found the Gospel the word and the will of God. I
second the resolutions.

The resolutions were unanimously adopted, and the Secretary requested to forward a copy of the same to the family
of the deceased